SPLIT HAIRS

To
G.S.G.

Je suis la plaie et le couteau!
Je suis le soufflet et la joue!
Je suis les membres et la roue,
Et la victime et le bourreau!

from *les Fleurs du Mal*
Baudelaire

Contemporaries
Robert Hazel, Editor

SPLIT HAIRS

by

Wende Locke

New York University Press
New York   1970

CONTENTS

A Block of Trees   7
Midday Reflection
Transfusion   9
Lizzards have a way of changing death into a color   11
Like the Seventh Veil   12
Split Hairs   14
. . . Autumn   15
The Convict   16
The Milkman   18
Hey, Mr. America   19
Margin   21
The Presentation   22
Will what's inside you ever come out?   24
Apocalypse   26
To Lazarus (in search of a tale)   27
A disease of exile has covered the world   28
The Lesson   30
The Explosion   31
Connection   33
To an Old Woman Dying in London   34
Collage   36
My Season   37
You stare into the spaces now   38
There are doors that open in the sky   40
Night Doorman   42
Freeing Myself into Madness   44
Mirrored   45
Revelation   46
The Grey Faces   47
The Sacrifice   50
Upon the Entrance of U.S. Troops into Cambodia. . . .   52
The Museum   54
Somnambulist   56

Rain Song   58
Magic Feet   59
Mono in Spring   61
The One-legged Trump   63
The Year of the Stars   64

A BLOCK OF TREES

They are lined up like prisoners
Ready to be identified behind a
Screen of windows.

I see thirty if I see one,
A tribe of analogues waiting for a face.
I will draw it on for them.

A block of trees.
They stand wide as a smile
Outside my flat they perch

Tall and straight like a band of Hessians.
They are not for climbing;
They are on display.

They wear the sky
Like a flap, over their bony handles,
Fingers reaching out in highways through the clouds.

Shaking out their leaves like flea-bit mutts,
They fold in and out like curtains
And a green wallpaper paints my street.

I mustn't breathe too hard
They might retreat,
Leaving me the inside of neighbors'

Lives, to peer at from my window.
The trees are something special.
Something for a birthday or a wedding.

I will marry them
And stretch my rubber skin up to their swollen sky.
Stepping from my window like a virgin leaf

Green and dew-struck
I spill into their arms;
We run together

Like colors, blending in a flush
Of whispering
I do. I do. I do.

MIDDAY REFLECTION

Watering the afternoon,
I wade through
The design of hours,
Tasting waves of thought.

I am not your demi-god.
No primeval spirit from the dead;
But a periscope. Clear-reflecting
Image of your wasting dream.

Atrophied. Dying from a lack of
Marrow. I become a bird with hollow bones;
Flying-yaffle. Winged thing.
Omens wear well on me.

I cannot feel my wings.
Do they carry me back to myself
Into my kind of mirror.
Or is this afternoon inside the mirror, after all.

TRANSFUSION

"They wax old as a garment;
the moth shall eat them up"
Isaiah, i,9

I am eighty years of transfusion
Eighty samples of given blood—
Pure as kleenex
I slip out of myself
Pale as a faint.
I put on my blood like a new face
And wear it out into the world,
The blood cells wander into the test tube undisturbed
This year is bigger than most—
It grows inside my belly like a fetal-fungus,
Holding on. Holding on.
Twenty geraniums on my window sill,
A present from the neighbor's child,
The warlock's son—
His knees circle me with their stare,
Myopic knees bulging at the bone.
He will devour me in the fall!
I call the Healer.
If he is Svengali, I know his terms.
He lives next to me in off hours.
He sleeps inside me
He will be my next child.
I will call for help and he will deliver himself
When I am in labor.
I call . . . the wolves return
Packing me off;
The empty horn,
It sounds and sounds.
I ring the bell,
The gong

9

Screaming to be heard.
He appears
He holds onto his stiff smile like a stolen gift,
It wears him out.
He takes my arm in a tourniquet clutch
Looking for the spot that might contain fresh cells,
The vampire overwhelms him—
He pricks and waits . . .
Warlock, warlock I cannot clot!
I am chaste as a snowdrop—
I am young. I am no tube of years.
It is only the blood that has aged
Only blood. Only blood.

LIZZARDS HAVE A WAY OF CHANGING DEATH
INTO A COLOR

Lizzards have a way of changing death into a color.
Creeping on vanilla stomachs,
Stripping off one skin to let another in

They've found a way for dying.
They do it to renew each time.

With each new skin they
Masquerade from Monk to Indian

And in a reflex they are free,
Shedding one life for another.

I've watched them die into a different skin,
I've watched the movements they begin
A dancing to the sun.

I know no way to equal theirs;
All other deaths are permanant.

My many skins lay one on top another,
Layered to the marrow of my bones.

My padding cannot peel away with seasons,
My death is not so easy.

> " 'Exist' and 'die' are just words,
> figments of our imagination.
> Tear your prison bars aside and
> batter down the walls! Escape from
> definitions and you will breathe again."
>
> *Exit the King*, Ionesco

My eyes burn in at me,
Two balls of sun
Peeling me down with the night.
My lungs, iron and chunky
Clink like two dungeon doors
Pushing their way in and out.
It is the night,
The horrors of black that winds
Its velvet through my brain.
I quake,
Lava falls through my veins
Strumming my insides out with a blackness
So pure it smothers.
Like a bruised peacock,
Head turned in its feathers,
I hide.
I am feather-fragile.
The night that should bring slumber
Does not comfort me.
My dreams,
A tower of babel inside my head,
Grow like a lightbulb from my neck.

O wizard,
Bring me Alf's button, Solomon's seal,
Aladin's lamp.

Bring me colors of silk,
Waves:
Long silver locks
I can fly off on.
Melt me into bubbles and float me out
Into the world like a star.
Or, if there is something
More, something bigger
Than magic,
Let it steal through me
Like the seventh veil,
Unknown and mysterious,
Swollowing up the division of night and day,
All beginnings, all endings . . .
Coming to me as a lover,
Waltzing me through the world on his shoulders.

SPLIT HAIRS

You say that
Love is
    like a split hair

Doubled
And bound to
    one root.

How thin
The anaemic fiber
    that you say is

Purer than a thousand virgins,
Peonies blushing through
    their pumpkin smiles.

You say that
It is growing always like a Eucalyptus
    branching out above the sky.

How distant are the branches
How separate are its leaves
    the ground is lonely for the feel of them

Dull bark is all it knows.
And what of
    love,

Linked by a Siamese foot,
Climbing up
    in all directions

Worn out with growth.
Collapsing far
    far from where it sprung.

The swollen veins
Of leaves,
Dew-happy and
Varicose
March into our hair and
Climb down our bodies
Not like catipillars
Inch by inch
But in a sparkle,
A recognition.
The spell of autumn
Screams its weird magic
Flashing a haunt of bright teeth
In a spell.
From Kensington Pond,
To Queen Ann's Park,
Down through Picadilly
The ritual marches.
The season knows its way—
It follows
Even from a distance.
A blanket-woman,
Veiled in the smog of Circe,
I am cast in and out of
A secret,
Telling me
To believe only
In what cannot be
Summoned
Into extinction.

THE CONVICT

I.

It is Siberia here
This cold cold workcamp of my soul.

Crippled in frost-bite
I do my time. My robot

Body dragging me from chore to chore.
And that Lucifer whip you hold above my head

Has frozen like an Eskimo's smile
Upon my back. Sticking

Sticking to my skin like sap.
Where do you lead me next

What chain gang pulling me back and forth
Like a curtain or a crowded métro.

With my paraffin lamp and my woolen underwear
I can follow any climate.

I can wind around the clock and never stop
For time or digging graves.

Nothing matters in the winter of my gut,
Filling up and spitting out like lungs,

I move on and motion has no recollection;
All is in the present. And my many selves

Dissolving with the seasons,
Renew and die in rhythm.

It is voodoo, this shaman spirit calling me
To war.

Walpurgisnacht.
And the stormtroopers are anywhere;

Auschwitz, Buchenwald, Terezienstadt.
A Devil's Island of glass boxes

Strung together like inches.
Windowless.

Choking me as I move
From camp to camp.

These ghetto padlocks clinking monotone as I walk.
What new penal settlement handcuffs my soul.

The choice is endless the prisoners beyond count.
Does Pluto cast his spell upon the world?

The hobby-horse sways back and forth in desperation;
The freight train jumps its track and falls

Into a coma on its side.
All is quiet. All is cotton.

And my patient jailor bounces his keys like a yo-yo,
Waiting for the prison break.

THE MILKMAN

He comes with the morning,
Starless. Bringing
In another day.

Routed. He opens up the day;
A cypress, offering his twigs
Bottled white as hospital sheets

Spread out to dry in the sun.
A travesty. Opaque
Imitations of his wares.

He arrives shuffling
His bottles; they organ-grind
A simple tune. A heart murmur.

He stops at my door,
Dutiful as a lapdog retrieving a bone.
Everyday the same

Uniformed in grey tulle
Shabby from abuse, he always knows the way.
I stopped him yesterday to see if he could speak

I asked him for the time.
As if a sun-dail were attached inside his nose
He took a breath big as his body

Letting out the air in one burst
He answered, "nine-thirty, ma'am."
It didn't seem to matter if he told it right.

Funny man. Milking his way through each day
Like a habit.
Revolving mandrel. He will never stop.

HEY, MR. AMERICA

Buffalo Bill in a glass
Screened T.V.
Romeo of the opera
Collapsing the trees with your
Wink—
Back straight, head arched,
Feet lighter than a tear
Hop-a-long riding the Indians
Back to the fort.

Hey, Mr. America, you ain't no Gary Cooper,
After all.
But a fudge cake, a
Mounds bar, a Mickey Mouse watch.
I've got you timed, pinned down
And tied on to yourself
Tighter than a shrunken girdle.

You pound your ulcer with two quarts
Of milk
That you stole from the cat,
Convinced that your scars are proof of
The ten gallon hat.

Lift it . . . up . . . just a little
Higher.
Ah, your electrons are splitting
Your scalp, and thining
That though fuzzy crown
That blows round your head.

In fact, you've balded a beautiful
Tan. Sunk into your skin and decided
To stay there.
You are yesterday's news, tomorrow's
Crisis . . .
But today, we will pickle you
And hold you
Out for ten cents a peek.

A puffed out tire
Riding your belt,
You lie on your back now,
An old bottle of Schlitz,
Flat and silly
With no kick but the stale yellow
Coloring,
The lost sparkle of taste.

MARGIN

Too distant in the still,

We stand too brief
    Too far.

In herds we stand

As ladders tempting walls
    To fall upon our steps

To separate our limping hands.

Our branches stretching
    Heavy

Into roots we gaze.

Ground to ground
    We form in stalks

And fan our faces with the spray of

Distance:
    Clothing for the space between our frames.

THE PRESENTATION

I am explosive

Don't come any closer or
I'll blow you up with

The world, is dying idly anyhow,

So what's another life?
Slow death was never in your palm.

Lean over here and I'll whisper my

Blood-burst
Grenade into your ear

Phoning in a drone around the earth.

Do you dare accept my gift?
Or are you paralytic like the sky

Stuck in the same spot unable to move near me.

It only stings for a little while
And no more than the world stings you now.

You are frightened;

I see you folding backwards
Like the sea, you flush in and out with

Indecision.

I will wrap it for you—
In freckled colors

You will light up

Like a spotted volcano;
We could say that it was Christmas

Then you'd understand a present.

With your ears blindfolded and your eyes plugged
You would approach,

And with a home-sick moan you would

Fly back through the sky.
Hurry up before I change into a star.

WILL WHAT'S INSIDE YOU EVER COME OUT?

A limping kangaroo
In your starched gingham
Growing with your stomach
Stretching out to your nose,
You've grown double inside
Yourself.
A kite is flying in your womb—
Tied back to a part of you,
It tugs at a new freedom.
Will what's inside you ever come out?

Your legs grow thud-heavy,
Two sphinx sticks
Holding you up,
While in you a wild hoof
Impatiently butts
Through the night.

When you first lost your shape
It happened so simply,
A little lump under
The side of your waist.
We thought the baby
Would spring out of your hip.
But then the rivers opened up,
And spread inside you
Like a galloping wave,
You rocked back and forth
With delight.
Will what's inside you ever come out?

Your body is stuffed
Full with another world
A simple beauty:
The language of children.

It is renewal!
You will be born again
Giving birth.
A part of you will
Cut-open the world for
The first time.

When your legs open their petals
And a shriek of birth
Blows out in a drunk,
The splash of
A new pulse
Will paralyze the ears
Of the world.

APOCALYPSE

Hot red flames from the gut
And once again I count the music
Of fire—
One, two, jumping into the flames
At three—
Numbers to heaven
And the sky cracks at my
Lip-twitch.

It is the day of the owl,
The black ink of the seal,
Cold starless eyes
Of the moon have found me.
I will ride them like a torch
Golden-heavy on my back . . .

The whip, the whip
It shrieks under my skin
With a silver sun.

One, two, I will glide into the
Northern lights
And run to the glimmer of colors,
Aurora Borealis—
The child of light
Cradles himself
Tears his cord and

Breaks through
A sky of
Frenzied sparks,
Electric eruptions
Painting the shadow of the moon.

TO LAZARUS (IN SEARCH OF A TALE)

He spins his dangling limbs
In a ferris-wheel churn.
Circles in his circles
His mouth reaching out for the other end of him.
In touch with himself on every fling
He goes with his body in search of the whip
Lassoing round on his other end.
He hurtles, he sprints and catches up with
(from time to time)
The part of himself he cannot believe to be
Part of himself.
More of a God than a dog
Omnipotent in his will
Convinced of his power
And yet, how human he becomes—
Believer in nothing but what he sees,
  Knowing no more
  And wanting to know nothing else.
Content in his circles
Lost in his game
Following his needs
At every point:
  Stopping when he is tired
  And not caring why he began or why he gave up.
Created with nothing loftier than his whim.
Destined in his small destiny.

The black liquid of
Undefined mist
Swims down
Fresh cheeks with
The lost blood of dreams.
The stammering child
With the limping club foot
Knew it from birth,
And the two-headed freak stuck
In the zoo of display
Holds it out for the world
To see.

They stare up at
A roofless flutter
Of gulls scooping down by the
Pier, wide-winged
Children of hell,
Playmates of the sky—
Carpeting the sea for years
In a strange prison
Caught between the sheets of mirror
That glove the sun.
Flapping down at the sea,
They defy the large diamond
Winks of its waves.

The taste of water sizzles
Up a tall bridge
I stretch over.
It sprinkles me with a measure
Of my world.
The rooms of my universe are stamped

And sealed
With a cry of the outlaw,
Hooting through the abyss
Of sound.

Where is the day before
The day before the
Day
And why are the wicks of cold
Waves burning out . . .
They too are on trial.
A disease of exile
Has covered the world.
Pinned it back from itself
Holding it arms length from
A touch.
Even the dim truths
In the bumps of history
Have turned against the rhythm
Of things.

A century splits through me
The twitch of an eyelid
Breaks
The atmosphere in a strange blur.
Slumped over with the moon,
I curl into a vast wave—
Detaching the bones of memory
From the loose body of the sea.

THE LESSON

Little girl:
Black man, black man
How deep does color grow.
Is it underneath your scalp?
Between your teeth?
Blacker than a color, you've become
A giant cinder.
If I touch you will I burn?

Black man:
White child, white child
My color's in my blood.
My color's all around me
Like a halo, like a poultice.
If you touch me I will burn.

Little girl:
Black man, black man
Do you cry black tears
And bleed black blood?
Do you bruise black;
And does your brain have only black thoughts?

Black man:
White child, white child
I ache black all over.
My blood fades the blackest ink;
I cry tears blacker than a zebra's stripe.
But some say my thoughts are getting far too white.

THE EXPLOSION

It is all spilling out of me:
The iced wind,
The whore-moon,
The boxing ocean,
That sandbox, where I played
The days those tears first dripped
From the bark of the sun.
It is all opening out of me.
The spell of centuries is
Broken.

Yet, there is a slice of me still,
A little part of me
That I hold onto.
The Moby Dick in my soul,
Stronger and more invincible than
The rest of me . . .
I can't spit up that enduring part.
It holds onto itself in spite of itself.

The fisherman's line casts out from me
Once more,
Rebounds and hooks back into my
Last eyelet,
Ripping it raw as the gut that exploded.
But I am still not free of it.
Tattered, spitting out its last blood
It clutches to me like the
White buffalo to its mount.
Above the point of coming down,
Of dying, of living.

It is that last shiver
In the enormity of the sky,
The one last paraplegic shake
That still jerks its lightning through me.
The gut, the gut
Spits back at me in horror,
Looking for its last part.
It has the rest of me
There at its pulse-touch.
It picks at me like a hungry dog
At dead meat—
Swollowing me up with a guzzle,
Waiting hands at its feet in a beg.
Curled up and limp in front of me,
Wagging for its last treat,
My freedom
Slides down with the window.

CONNECTION

It is August in your eyes.
Sun beside the park

You trace the leaves in lemon.
Your magic wings unsnap

You fold in feathers
You climb.

It is Christmas in the sky;
Your eyes are out of season.

Let winter happen.
My paper skin

Strains into white confetti;
Snow falls from your eyes.

You have met my season.
Your eyes

Two glass balloons connecting
With my winter, leave August for the blind.

TO AN OLD WOMAN DYING IN LONDON

You are dying now.
Arthritic like your peeling ceiling
Your skin is flaking off in leprosy.
You are melting like a vapour.

Your mind has lost its center.
Your prejudices have become bloodspots
On your brain.
Go back into your skin

Like a turtle
And do your dying alone.
I will not accompany you;
We will each do it separately.

Your crippled frown has sunk through your mouth
Like wax, it drips between your teeth.
And your little dog,
Flipping back and forth like a Mexican bean

Knows that someone's had it.
He sits by the stove now
Hoping that you might
Speed up the process by a whiff of fumes.

His stomach swells at the smell of you.
Dead flesh inside his jaw.
You are alone in the country of dying.
Alone to feel yourself

Begin to loose yourself.
You might have taken your life half a century back,
But you had to wait for it to take you
And all your mean tricks

Which were forgiven when you passed seventy.
I whittled you down to a shred of bark
And buried you in my sandbox some eons ago—
You cannot call my name now,

You cannot have me at your dying.
For God's sake get it over with and leave me alone.

COLLAGE

Lying head by head
Like a collage,
Pieced together and stuck on to ourselves
Like false eyelashes—
Blink and I will disappear.

You move and I feel you
Folding up in this double coffin.
I touch you and assure myself that,
Spread out next to me
Like a thousand ghosts of a thousand faces,

You are by my side;
A window face—
Our steel framed lips:
Metal connecting magnet,
Instinctive gravitation.

What serpent have I brought to my bed?
Bloodless. Cold without knowing
That you never reached me.

Or could it be,
That you are my Lancelot,
My saviour.
My God! Knowing all
Hiding your thoughts in a pillow of white snow.

MY SEASON

Does it come in spring with strings of tulips
Pouting at the thought of fall?
Does it come in winter with armadillos
Clothed in bony armor,
Snuggling up inside themselves to keep warm?
Does it come with death—
Still and unremembered.
Or is it in the motor of some sluggish tugboat,
Chugging off to no where.

It is impervious, it stops
Here at my feet, it rubs
Against my cactus body like a pond of silk.

Miasma: circles of swelling.
It is choking me in it python coils.
Will it show itself?
Can it stop for me like Christmas,
Every year on time—
Giftwrapped with anticipation
I enter it,
Turning
Round in it with compass-eyes.

It is a flaming veil,
My season: Batiushka,
Priest of the wind,
Cycloning from a dream.

YOU STARE INTO THE SPACES NOW

You stare into the spaces now,
Living in a solitary sphere.
Moon-gazing,
Sky-struck
In your thick Morris chair, you sit
Alone now in a private midnight.

You sip your tea at the usual time,
Ride off in your pin-striped suit
To dine;
But your smile is no sun-spot
Anymore, you have taken the glow
Inside you,
In the dull-spangled
Light of old age.

You are polarized,
Neutral as yogourt,
Pure and simple.
There was a time
When the days were toasted
In dazzle.
Repose didn't know you—

Tender paladin,
Strange knight,
Now you are tucked into the days.
They cover you up in a veil,
A windshield,
Blinking you through time
In a frieze.

Where are the days of deeringdo,
The unshakable nerve holding on
To the challenge of hope.
Your large hands, stiffened
To a sag,
Now fold at your side
Like feathers unplugged
In a quiver.

Soldier of fortune,
You once solved the problems of a day
Or a century, in a few velvet words.
But today, you are being lived—
You ride the current like a dream,
Giving into its own way of logic.

This quiet force that takes you
Is a queer planet,
Hooded and glazed.
A smokey film sheets your days.
A prescription for peace,
The calm wonder
Of the aging star
You hold on to.

THERE ARE DOORS THAT OPEN IN THE SKY

> "... And silence like a poultice
> comes to heal the blows of sound."
> O. W. Holmes, 'The Music Grinder'

I have swollowed a cry.
Its tubercular cough
Spits up from me
Like a forest fire
Consuming, consuming.
I stop it deep in me,
Hold onto its whisper in the night
And rock it to sleep.
But it escapes into the wind at dawn.
It once had a child,
A fetal-toy,
That grew in it with a golden-smoke.
But it killed it with shrill razor-thorns,
With its fascist-blade.
Now the cry has no shadow,
It is empty like an echo.

I took it to drink from the waters of Lethe,
Had it down to the underworld and
Brought it back
Screaming
With its perfume of blood
And soaring out of me like an empire.

There are doors that open in the sky,
Pockets of light
That reach out their arms.
If I could bind this cadence up,
Flush its frenzied sea-roar
Through the sky
Until it stood on top of the world
Like a star.
Then comes the beauty of clearness,
The tall mysteries of peace,
Sinking in a slumber, unaware of time
Or laughter, or dreams.
A silence so deep it purifies,
Sifting through the palest desert of centuries.
Comforting, comforting.
A gentle sigh, filling up the spaces of things.

NIGHT DOORMAN

Tall,
Impenetrable
He stands,
Playing at being a door.
A cartload of faces
Dribble in through his
Smile,
Closing behind it
In a slam.
The glass screen
He folds in and out like
A fan,
Blows a circle of
Evening guests
Over the doormat of
Opaque nights.

His song is a procedure.
Erect like a blade
Of grass in shock,
His shoulders drain
Down his sides
In a snuffed-out exhaust.
Bloodhound of the door,
Policing the nightmare hour—
Tied to his post
In a definition;
Holding back the shadows,
The furies,
The cry in the night.
He is bolted to his slot,
Tacked onto the address he has
Traded for home.

In the hunched cave of dusk,
Aching with the granite,
He slumps across the pavement
Of his act.
Ears growing large like a rabbit,
He nibbles pieces of gossip
For food.
Hearing all, he tells it
A different way—
For the hope of uncertainty,
The trick of surprise.
A churn of decades lowers
Its eyes to him
In oblivion.

FREEING MYSELF INTO MADNESS

If I let go of one rein
And let it ride
Free through a gallop,
There would be that second part
Of me
Remote and holding on.
But if I could lose both reins
In stampede
Through my hands,

I could free myself into madness—
Be carried off by the dust-shooting
Hooves;
By the sparklers, the music
The diaphamous veil.
Faster and faster the frenzy
Would churn me,
Milking me through a weightless
Tornado.
Thin of myself,
Loosing my guideposts, my landmarks
My birthmarks.
The small black mole on my left shoulder
Would be plucked off
And placed across my heart
In love.

This demon, this demon
That holds me back from myself
That clamps me down,
Slapping my wings into handcuffs,
Shutting me off from the air that I breathe,
Winding me into my skin like a mummy . . .

The baby's wail,
That birthslap into life,
Cries inside me like a trapped tear—
Gently, gently
Night has turned
My gasping clavicord
To clay.

MIRRORED

Into the steam
   Between twin toes
I milk my way
   Across a sky.

I see a seahorse
   Yawning pork into my eye.
It rides vertigo
   Upon my sleeve,

Flies in trot
   Onto the thinness of a cloud,
Travels down into
   The cabbage patching

Roots onto a
Multiplicity of feet.

45

REVELATION

No one dares turn over in his bed.
Asleep like mummies
Or groundhogs waiting for a better season—
A terrible still sways the air.

In the little brick church down the road
Some pagan priest is babbling oracles to the dead.
Dissenters lift up their coffins
Breathing in a new canon.

And up on the highest cliff
Some new power cradles a new god in its arms.
The pious sink into their skin like over-ripe fruit.
They do not know how to die.

I fall back upon my side
Like an expectant mother, swollen
With eyes open in slumber.
Knowing with each falling night,
My small life dies into its sleep.

THE GREY FACES

Faded,
Cracked, chipping off the words
Between stained-grey
Fangs, they feed
Us the thick lies of
War.

Barking
Their siren into our ears
Till we grow deaf with the cry
For death, for death.
Hollow and round like the globe they must sit on
To swollow, to plunder.

They have stuffed us with lye,
Cut us open with poison—
Hand-fed, spoon-fed
The diet of death.
Blood-struck cannibals of the state,
Sons of Hitler. They march on us

Shouting that love equals chauvinism;
They part their lips and
Launch out their tongues for it.

O captor, lend me your whip,
Your country, your nation.
O ruler, lend me your weapons,
Your guns and your tear-gas.
There is a crystal land across the bridge,
It wears a golden glow.

But the grey faces hear only echo.
The heavy-lidded, over-fed
Pythons of violence
Pounding the peace-drum,
Beating out the song of the kill.
In their grey uniforms they arrive

With their grey smiles pinned on,
Banana lips
Held stiff in their helmets of hate.

O God, if all the heros have died
And all the brave have failed
And all the world is standing on its head
Eating fire
And voodoo has given way to bullets,
Flat lead, eating four youths

Out of dreams,
The West will wrap itself in a panic—
The cold, empty howl of trapped wolves.
A shadow grows heavy in the spaces,
It turns in on us
Pointing long winding fingers if night—

Screaming down on the deaths at Kent State:
Four little cherubs,
Once bounced on two knees like balloons.

It stings the red faces, the blue faces
The faces of love—
Sick with the smell of it,
Cut open like lepers
Tasting corrosion,
Explosion.

O, plaster us up
Cast us in grey
Enamel.
Cut off our ears
Scoop out our eyes
Slice our bodies up for vermin,

But our hearts will tick on like Shelley's.
Our blood will ooze out and
Fight back with the daggers of ghosts.
Our souls, our marrow,
The gut of us
Will tick, tick, tick

Till the grey faces,
Those window-masks of death,
Have been haunted out of their skin.

THE SACRIFICE

The lambs will come
Will come and free us from our
Sanatoriums,
Our tired iron lungs on stretchers
Wait for their arrival.
They will come
Showing us the way to where we
Think to go
Or go to think.
They will come
Down the mountain flocking
At our feet in sacrifice,
To show us how it's done.
And when they come
And when they look up bleating in our eyes . . .
The shovel, the anvil, the tools
The tools to feed them to our God,
Our God who knows we cannot know the way it's done.
We move on instinct and burn them in the flames of
Sacrifice,
Burning with them;
Perceiving how it's done.
And the hell fires spit back
A sigh of thank you from beneath our feet.
The dying,
Earth-eaten, worming their way back up
The mountain in a breath of ash.
We see how they are made to bleed.
To bleed and free us from our sitting rooms,
Where we wait for them
To reenter by the midnight gong.
We fill the rooms with waiting.

And they return
In yards of fleece returning to our hospitals
Of death, returning
To our symbols, our icons, our effigies
Held above our heads like smoke-crowns
Or air; the air we toast them in
Our final thanksgiving, is at hand.
We stand hands out in welcome
Waiting still and still inside us,
About us. Over us
They cry and are heard.
   Hear us too in our salvation as we roast them for a soul.

UPON THE ENTRANCE OF U.S. TROOPS INTO CAMBODIA AND THE KILLINGS OF FOUR YOUTHS AT KENT STATE AND TWO ON JACKSON STATE CAMPUS

So what's in a lie?
Just a little white joke

To coax the anxious back to the state,
To hoax the angered back into line.
Lines to live by
Lines to fight by
Lines of lines
But what line to die by?

What slogan or trick
Can line back the dead,
What magic or word can bring back the
Slaughtered?
Six lumps of hope exploding
Under the passionate bullets
Of hate.

So what's in a lie?
Just a little white joke
A President's whim,
A Vice-President's nod,
While two campus co-eds
In search of the yellow God
In the sun of the East,
Are shot down by the Klu Klux Klan
Of our white little cabin on Capitol Hill.

O, lies become blacker,
Hate becomes sloppier,
Guardsmen butcher like Brown Shirts,
Sturmabteilung—
Their starving hands twitch at the trigger.
A poison bloats their veins
With the triumph of power.

So what's in a lie?
Just a little white joke . . .

Just a few lives,
Six young splintered
Death-cries,
And a few more
Lies,
That's all. That's all.

THE MUSEUM

Hollow as a mausoleum.
Faces weave their noses in and out of
Drafty rooms.
Snake-corridors, a winding silence.
There are ghosts here.

A grand woman in a starched face opens
Her compact mirror,
Gasping through the glass;
A herd of mummies circled up behind her
Look on with admiration.
Stopped by the *Metamorphosis of Narcissus*,
A crowd of hungry librarians read the answers
They have no time to find in books.
Their heads bob up and down in a handshake,
While an under-stuffed tonsured cleric

Creeps in front of them looking with hypnotic wonder;
His eyes move down the painting
Like salt through an hour glass.
He has three minutes for a look.
And in the corner a uniformed

Eunich paces up and down,
Watching over
The string of greedy feet
Moving round like drachmas
Spinning on the floor.

A hospital showroom—
With walls as clean as lightning,
Advertising free culture for everyone.
Back and forth like swinging doors
They walk. Looking and relooking

Over their shoulders
To see if anyone is looking with them.
An old man paralyzed in his wheelchair
Pushes his way through the smiles
To stop at his favorite picture: *Pope with Fan Canopy.*

He parks himself there like a polarized Goliath.
Lights flash off and on,
Thunder pounding in his eyes—
The rooms spill empty,
Rush-hour faces draining down the sink.

Alone in his gallery,
He hums the last refrain of "Leibestod" and
Closes himself up for the night.

SOMNAMBULIST

"We are near waking
When we dream we
are dreaming."
                            Novalis

Thump . . . on my mind
Each night the same.
Shh . . . the world is letting go,
The windows are slammed shut and
The goblin is snoring the lock off.
I climb down into myself like an old saddle
I ride, deep into my seat
I slide, until the falling slaps me in the face
And I wake grounded to my bed,
Screwed to my bed like a togglebolt.
Then back again I splash into
My private camera.
It is the desert now . . . a white sheet of crystal
Spread out in the sun like salt.
I am crossing a war, a battleground—
The enemy circles me like commissars,
We ring around each other
Trapped by our own rhythm.
It is Algiers I have to win and the enemy confounds me,
Closing in like a magnet—
I tear my skin off like a leper peeling his bark.
Layer by layer I go down into . . .
I slip down into, crawling the desert—
A sand-lizard.
On my stomach like an infant, a new puppy,
I have lost my spine.
It has gone into my head like a tumor
Grappling with my brain,
My fever cap.

I am hotter than the hell fires,
The thermometer has burst and
My blood runs wild—
Gunga Din screaming through the desert
Alone, the warriors have retreated.
I run after them hooting like an Indian.
And my body is like a colored map—
Each organ glowing to the sun.
Blue for liver, red for heart, green for marrow—
Uncovered. Naked like an X-ray.
Looking for my skin, my clothes,
I panic and the ground slips under me,
Folding in my body. Sucking me down through
A deep womb-tunnel.
I scream to hear an echo
But my voice has forgotten how to
Sound . . . I jump awake to the try,
Swallowing the night like Cronus' children.
Knowing that what I wake to is the dream.

RAIN SONG

Dangling rain
Dripping down my life
Like honey, sticking to my windowpane,
My memorypane.
Sliding with the rain

I become the dots of dandruff
Falling from the bald sky-head,
Raining in on me,
Melting me into the pavement,
The cobbles of a dream.

I carry the rain like a tear
Heavy inside me.
A fetus dropped from the belly of a cloud,
Like speckled neon, I float—
Loose confetti of the world.

Falling softly through my mind,
I drift to ground.
Grounded to earth like stilts, I stand
Wooden. Rooted.
I am the drop that has landed

Looking up at the sky in question.
I ask it to carry me back to where I came from
To the scalp of my source.
Traveling salesman of the sky,
Wisping through the open skyland,

Fall through life like an old Caruso record.
Archaic. Spinning round and round
On my self-propelled disk.
A sky-drop raining down in thunder,
As the world shakes out of me.

MAGIC FEET

"I am myself a criminal because
I kill the mind. I do not want
thought, I want wisdom."
                    Vaslav Nijinsky, *Diary*

Madman,
        beggarman
At the saint-gate of hell.
    Pirate,
        Pope of
The secret universe you sell.
    Blackman,
        Blueman,
            Greenman,
    White
        man as pure as the coal paint of night.

Nijinsky
    Nijinsky
The namesake,
The birthmark—
    The blood leaks
        grave-grey on your stone,
While the epyleptic foot
    dancing over your tomb,
        taps out
A cold epitaph of winter.

Madman,
        beggarman
Prophet of dreams—
    The ballet, the dream-step
    The music, the soul-step

Steps
    you leaped
        out of
    To be the dance not the dancer
    The notes not the player
    The dream not the vision.

High, higher than
    Tall
Canopes of leaves
    that you melted
               downstage on.
Your eagle-feet flipping
    you through air like a wing.
Releasing your lightning,
        your magic,
        your demon.

O, how did the world destroy you?

    There is a mob
    Of killers
Hanging our their bones on a cross.

    Your hangmen
    stand,
        forehead pulled over their eyes
in a think.
    Your hangmen
    stand,
        hands crippled and swollen
with the liquid of murder.
    They'll kill again
in your recall,
    your keepsake.

Nijinsky,
　　Nijinsky
A part of you
　　still dangles music
through the tall sky of oaks,
　　hypnotising
　　　　　　leaves
　　　　　　　　off.

MONO IN SPRING

The killer in me,
That old hooved and curdled
Laugh that bobs and grows
Inside my blood,
Reaching boiling point
And holding back like the trick
Of a summer shower,
Sweats a little and then
Gives off an electric glow
Of fever-beams.

It is so hot in here.
The fever that brought spring
With it
Scorches those overcooked beads
Of love that fall off my brow
Like magicians,
Tumbling into each other and
Disappearing
In the pillow I drown in.

The soft drape that draws my window,
The distance of the seasons—
Into its grip like an old friend,
Grows heavy
More sweaty and less sure of the month.
But the waves are singing
Somewhere in my gut,
And I know it must be spring.

Crawling back into my four-postered tomb,
Dull and virginal like the stars
That tune me into night . . .
It grows like an oven inside my skin—
Thick and consumptive,
Knocking me out with its promise
Of pureness.
I will bake to ginger
And be turned out for the pidgeons
To plunder,
(Those guiltless songs of Venice—impregnable).

The fat breeze at my window lies stiff on me,
Flat and used up
Like the whore on her back
In an attic loft on 14th Street.
And the days
Tick off me like old skin,
Peeling me out with the minutes,
Dripping me out and
Squeezing me through.
Starched and dizzy,
Winding time around inside my pocket
Like a washed out penny,
Under-exposed,
The albino days
Fade into my tatooed skin.

THE ONE-LEGGED TRUMP—Garcia Lorca

for Tom, in exile . . . "Venceremos."

Do you like the edges of things?
The straining of spaces
Stretching up to a tower, a spiral,
A point?
And the open wound that meets you
Like a womb,
Scalding with passion and pain?
Does your blood bubble inside you—
Lucifer's death dance
Pounding your pulse like a bongo
Drumming your insides out with its song.

If you have no stage that holds you
And wear yourself like a package string
Around the world,
The struggle, the travel, the caravan
Will take you
To the spirit of Lorca
Howling out through the winds
Of Toledo . . .
Beckoning,
Tempting you into
A new kind of Eden
Where death is a challenge
And sin a reward;
Where solace is found
In the secret of wonder.

THE YEAR OF THE STARS

The sky
Holds onto its stars
Like a puppeteer,
Pulling each twinkle of light
And letting it loose
Into the tunnel of original blue.
I watch it from my window,
The tall canopy of silk
Drifting in the womb of time.
The child that springs from the sky
Is not the child of any mother form,
But the newest infant of an age
That cannot conceive of birth
Or death.
An age of miracles—
Of silver shadows,
Celestial patterns,
Dancing in the spaces of things.
It is the year of the stars,
The golden birthday
Of the sun.
And eyes see their way to
The end of the sky,
Into worlds not yet explored,
Time not traveled through.
A stretch of the hand,
Infinity reaches out of a finger.